Writing-House Ducky

To Louise
—E.B.

To Emma and Kadin
—D.W.

Photography of cut-paper illustrations by Studio One

Text copyright © 1997 by Eve Bunting • Illustrations copyright © 1997 by David Wisniewski • The illustrations for this book were executed in cut paper (Color-Aid and Canson papers as well as textured plexiglass and Form-X film). The text was set in 18-point Helvetica Rounded. • All rights reserved. • For information about permission to reproduce selections from this book, write to Permissions, Houghton Mifflin Harcourt Publishing Company, 215 Park Avenue South, New York, NY 10003. • www.houghtonmifflinbooks.com • This Center for the Collaborative Classroom edition is published by arrangement with Houghton Mifflin Harcourt Publishing Company. • Center for the Collaborative Classroom, 1001 Marina Village Parkway, Suite 110, Alameda, CA 94501 • 800.666.7270 ∗ fax: 510.464.3670 • collaborativeclassroom.org • ISBN 978-1-61003-183-7 • Printed in China

6 7 8 9 10 RRD 20 19 18

Ducky

Written by **Eve Bunting**

Illustrated by **David Wisniewski**

Center for the Collaborative Classroom

I am a yellow plastic duck and I am in great danger.

Yesterday I was snuggled safe with hundreds of other bathtub toys. We were in a crate on a big ship.

A storm came.

Our crate was washed overboard.

DOWN

DOWN

DOWN it went.

We tumbled around inside,
yellow ducks, green frogs, blue
turtles, and red beavers.

BUMP

CRASH!

We hit bottom, the crate broke, and we bobbed
like colored bubbles to the surface.

The sun is rising now and the sea is pink.
My bathtub friends float all around me.
Our ship has disappeared.
The sea is big, big, big.
Oh, I am scared!

Fish with watery eyes come to stare.
A sea snake wiggles itself among us.
A great monster head rises close to me.

SHARK!

I go from scared to terrified.

The shark's mouth opens and it gulps in a frog, two beavers, three turtles, and me.

Things and bits of things are stuck in its giant teeth.

PFUH!

It shakes its head and spits us out. I expect we are not too tasty, though we are guaranteed non-toxic.

I wish we could swim and get away. But all we can do is float.

It is a relief when the shark goes.

A wedge of pelicans flies above us.
Oh, how I wish I could fly! I'd fly to safety.
The frog next to me is turned upside down
by a wave, then right side up by another.

But we are drifting far from one another.
Great sea spaces separate us.
  High on a sea swell I see us spread across
the ocean for miles and miles.

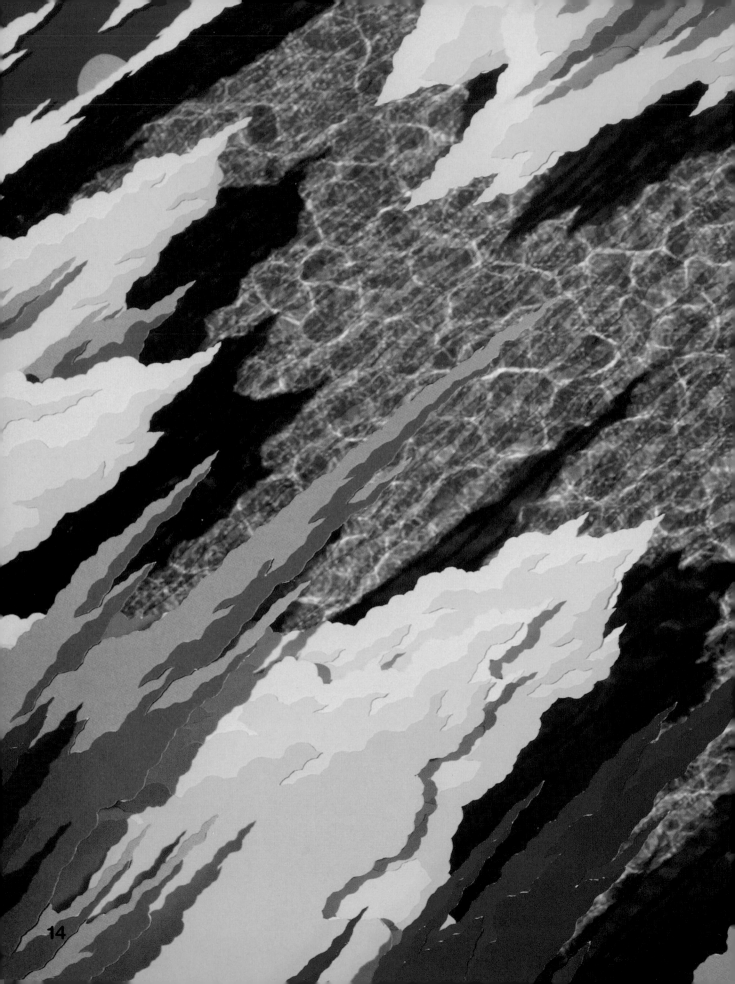

The next morning I have no yellow ducks, green frogs, blue turtles, or red beavers to keep me company. Like the ship, they have left, and I am alone.

I can't tell how long I float on the big,
empty ocean.

There are days when sun sparks the water.
When the ocean is blue with white ruffles.

There are days when I float through rain.

Days when wind blows me backward, tumbling me like a yellow ball. It is all the same to me. I only know the loneliness. There are days when fog hides me even from myself. Then I am lonelier than ever.

There are nights of clouds and nights of constellations.
There is a moon, and another and another.
The water must be colder now.
Ice nudges me.
Seals bark as I go by.
Will I float in this ocean forever and ever?

It is on a day of pale light that I feel the sea lift me, carry me, crash me down.

I'm somersaulting over small stones.

What is happening to me now?

Someone is shouting. "I've found one! I've found one! It's a duck!"

A boy's face is close to mine. We are nose to beak, beak to nose.

Another boy rubs my head. "Hi, Ducky!"

"That's what I'll call him, Ducky," my boy says.

His friend grins. "Good name. Very original."

"I need to report that I found him," my boy says. He gets on a bike. "Mrs. James is keeping a record for science."

For science? Me?

My gosh! Look at this!
It's great to see so many of my friends again.

Now we are in a room. My boy sets me on a table.

"I found him down on the beach, Mrs. James," he tells a woman.

"Thank you for reporting it," she says. She writes in a notebook. "I'll put it on my 'ducks found' list. People are finding a lot of these bathtub toys around town. The scientists are so interested."

"Ducky's coming home with me," my boy says.

We ride to his house and he puts me in his bathtub.

Oh, I am so happy!

I am a bathtub duck, fulfilling my destiny.

How wondrous it is to be able to float!

Author's Note

In 1992, a crate containing 29,000 plastic bathtub toy animals left on a ship from Hong Kong, China, bound for Tacoma, Washington, U.S.A. It was washed overboard in a storm. Hundreds of the toys have since been found, beached on the eastern coast of the Gulf of Alaska. Scientists are checking findings and sightings to learn more about currents, winds, and tides. Using computers, they plot the track of the remaining toys. Some, they believe, will go into the Arctic Ocean and ride a course toward the North Pole. Some could sail around the top of the world to the North Atlantic. One lone duck has been found off Washington State. How wondrous it is to be able to float!